Forgiveness

T H E R A P Y

Forgiveness
T H E R A P Y

Written by
David W. Schell

Illustrated by
R. W. Alley

GODSFIELD
PRESS

Copyright © 1995 *Godsfield Press Ltd*

Text © 1995 *David W. Schell*

Illustrations © 1995 *R. W. Alley*

Originally published in the US by Abbey Press 1987

Published in the UK by Godsfield Press Ltd 1995

Cover Design by *The Bridgewater Book Company Ltd*

ISBN 1 899434 50 X

Write to

GODSFIELD PRESS LTD

Bowland House

off West Street, Alresford

Hants SO24 9AT

The right of *David W. Schell* and *R. W. Alley* to be identified
as author and illustrator of this work has been asserted by them in
accordance with the Copyright, Designs and Patents Act 1988

A CIP catalogue record for this book is available
from the British Library

Printed and bound in the UK

Foreword

In his most popular work, *Mere Christianity*, C.S. Lewis wrote, "Everyone says forgiveness is a lovely idea until they have something to forgive...." Unfortunately, when we need its healing power most, forgiveness may seem neither a lovely idea nor an empowering one—only elusive, at best. And so, victimized once by whatever wrongs were done to us, we victimize ourselves again and again by allowing anger to take up residence in and drain vitality from our souls.

Life is a wonderful gift to be treasured and shared. But anger and resentment, fed by a refusal to forgive, block healing and growth. The gift becomes damaged—and all of us lose.

The thirty-five axioms in *Forgiveness Therapy* are inspired by the author's book, *Getting Bitter or Getting Better: Choosing Forgiveness for Your Own Good*. They can guide you through those times when your desire for vengeance seems to overshadow the power of love. They can help you find your own God-given emotional and spiritual strength to avoid bitterness and arrive at forgiveness.

Use and practice the axioms. Struggle with some, have fun with others—as you grow in celebrating your life as the greatest of all gifts.

1.

Forgiveness means bending without breaking, being strong enough to withstand the heavy weight of injury but resilient enough to recover. Be forgiving!

2.

Life is never perfect and often unfair. Forgive life's inevitable failures.

3.

Forgive yourself: for what you regret doing and for what you wish you had done, for not being fully yourself and for being only yourself.

4.

Self-forgiveness cleanses the soul, washing away shame and guilt. Out of self-forgiveness comes the power to extend forgiveness to others.

5.

You have the right to feel sad, betrayed, angry, resentful when you've been injured. Understand, accept, and express your feelings. Pushing them below the surface only means they will erupt in another place, at another time.

6.

Confront those who have hurt you; tell them how you feel. When that's impossible or when that could harm you or someone else, speak to them in your imagination.

7.

Forgiveness does not mean
accepting further abuse or
continuing destructive
relationships. Establish
boundaries for what is
acceptable to you and make
those boundaries clear to others.
Hold them accountable for
their actions.

8.

Justice may right the wrongs,
but forgiveness heals the hurt.
Seek forgiveness beyond justice.

9.

Sometimes people hurt you because, like you, they are learning and growing. Forgive their incompleteness, their humanness.

10.

To refuse to forgive is to continue to hurt yourself. Victimized once, your lack of forgiveness keeps you stuck as a victim, holding on to a victim's identity. Instead, claim the identity of one who forgives.

11.

Recognize how you've refused to forgive. Keeping inner monsters at bay requires energy. Instead, use your energy to affirm and embrace life.

12.

Victims are helpless, at the mercy of the offender. By showing mercy _to_ an offender, you put yourself back in control. Take charge by forgiving.

13.

Know that forgiveness is possible even in the most hurtful circumstances, even toward someone you may not trust or respect, even when someone doesn't seem to deserve forgiveness. It is a testimony to the goodness your Creator instilled within you from the first moment of your being.

14.

Forgiveness is the only real prescription for the pain you feel over someone else's behavior. The healing choice is yours to make.

15.

Think of forgiveness as a powerful survival skill. It helps you find your way through the wilderness of misunderstanding, hurt, resentment, and hatred.

16.

If you find it hard to forgive your parents for their imperfect parenting, remember: they were shaped by the imperfect parenting <u>they</u> received from parents who were shaped by their <u>own</u> parenting, and so on and so on...

17.

Forget about forgetting an injury. That's not always possible—and maybe at times not even desirable. Rather, choose to move on, past remembering to forgiveness.

18.

Let forgiveness be the catalyst
for a healthy chain reaction.
Forgiveness sterilizes the wound,
which permits healing, which
releases energy for growth.

19.

No loving relationship is free of hurts. Bind up the wounds of love with forgiveness.

20.

No offense is unforgivable—
unless you make it so. Use your
power wisely.

21.

When you are having a difficult time forgiving, recall a moment when you wanted to be forgiven. Offer the other person what you wanted to receive.

22.

Forgiveness takes practice. Start with small hurts and work your way up to the big ones.

23.

Forgiveness is a lifelong process. Forgive over and over—even for the same offense.

24.

Forgiveness may seem futile when you see no immediate results. But healing and growth are like fine aged cheese—not instant mashed potatoes. Give forgiveness time.

25.

No one can make you feel bad.
You have the power to choose
between getting bitter and
getting better. Take
responsibility for your
feelings; claim your power.

26.

You cannot change someone for the better by holding a grudge. Grudges only change <u>you</u>—for the worse.

27.

Ask yourself whether "I can't forgive" means "I won't forgive." Then turn your heart toward the warmth of God's love and allow that love to thaw your heart.

NO
CHERRY
PICKING

28.

Forgiveness takes courage and determination. Dig deep and you will find the strength you need.

29.

Allow forgiveness to open the door to reconciliation. Today's bully could be tomorrow's friend.

30.

Accept the possibility of rebuilding a relationship. Past offenses can be bulldozed and buried and a better life built atop the debris.

31.

Don't put conditions on your forgiveness, or your inner peace will depend on the decision of the person who hurt you. Make your own choice.

32.

When someone won't forgive
you, refusing to forgive in return
is no answer. That's like
wrapping yourself in the other's
chains. Keep yourself free;
forgive.

33.

To help you forgive, picture the other person surrounded by the light of God. See yourself stepping into that same light, and feel God's presence with you both.

34.

Forgive even when there has been no apology or restitution. If you withhold forgiveness until a wrong is made right, you risk condemning yourself to a life sentence of unresolved bitterness; you risk letting your life be shaped by someone else's actions.

35.

Forgiveness is not something you do for someone else; it is something you do for yourself. Give yourself the gift of forgiveness.

A psychotherapist in Selma, Alabama, **David W. Schell**, Ed.D, leads workshops on forgiveness and is the author of *Getting Bitter or Getting Better*, an Abbey Press book.

Illustrator for the Abbey Press Elf-help Books, **R.W. Alley** also illustrates and writes children's books. He lives in Barrington, Rhode Island, with his wife and daughter.

Elf-help Books . . . adding "a little character" and a lot of help to self-help reading!